THE GERMAN BATTL
GNEISENAU

SIEGFRIED BREYER

SCHIFFER MILITARY HISTORY

West Chester, PA

SELECT BIBLIOGRAPHY

Breyer: *Schlachtschiffe und Schlachtkreuzer 1905-1970*, Munich 1970.

Breyer, *Grosskampfschiffe 1905-1970, Vol. I*, Munich 1977.

Breyer-Koop, *Von der Emden zur Tirpitz, Vol. I*, Munich 1980.

Campbell, *Naval Weapons of World War Two*, London 1985.

Dulin-Garzke, *Battleships, Vol. III: Axis and Neutral Battleships in World War Two*, Annapolis 1985.

Gröner, *Die deutschen Kriegsschiffe 1815-1945, Vol. I*, Munich 1982.

Hadeler, *Kriegsschiffbau*, Darmstadt 1968.

Hildebrand-Röhr-Steinmetz, *Die deutschen Kriegsschiffe, Vol. II*, Herford 1980.

Hümmelchen, *Die deutschen Seeflieger 1939-1945*, Munich 1976.

Kähler, *Schlachtschiff Gneisenau*, Herford 1979.

Rohwer-Hümmelchen, *Chronik des Seekrieges 1939-1945*, Oldenburg 1968.

Schmalenbach, *Die Geschichte der deutschen Schiffsartillerie*, Herford 1968.

Schmalenbach, *German Battleships Scharnhorst and Gneisenau*, London, no date.

PHOTO CREDITS

Breyer collection: pp. 1, 3, 7, 10, 11, 12, 14, 15 (2), 19, 20 (2), 21, 26, 27, 29 (2), 36, 37, 38, 47 (3).
Federal Archives: pp. 12, 21, 25, 29, 30 (3), 31 (3), 32, 35 (2).
Royal Navy: P.48.
Dressler collection: pp. 4, 7, 13, 33 (2).
L. & L. Van Ginderen: P.42.
Gröner: P.33.
Hoheisel collection: P.35.
Koop collection: pp. 3, 4, 7, 9, 13 (2), 14, 23 (3), 24 (2), 25 (2), 28 (3), 36 (2), 37 (2), 39 (2).
Schäfer-Kiel: pp. 15, 16, 17, 18.
Schmalenbach: P.8.
Terzibaschitsch: pp. 42, 43 (2), 44 (2)

Ship sketches and detail drawings: Copyright S. Breyer.
Plan drawings pp. 26-27: Federal Archives-Military Archives.

Translated from the German by Dr. Edward Force, Central Connecticut State University.

Copyright © 1990 by Schiffer Publishing Ltd.
Library of Congress Catalog Number: 90-62989.

Printed in the United States of America.
ISBN: 0-88740-290-9

This title was originally published under the title, *Schlachtschiff "Gneisenau"*, by Podzun-Pallas-Verlag GmbH, 6360 Friedberg 3 (Dorheim).
ISBN: 3-7909-0314-0.

We are interested in hearing from authors with book ideas on related topics.

Published by Schiffer Publishing, Ltd.
1469 Morstein Road
West Chester, Pennsylvania 19380
Please write for a free catalog.
This book may be purchased from the publisher.
Please include $2.00 postage.
Try your bookstore first.

CONSTRUCTION HISTORY

The long-range plans of the German Navy included a future total of five "armored ships", that type that had come into being through the restricting conditions of the Treaty of Versailles and had gained the originally ridiculing name of "pocket battleship" outside Germany, only being regarded as opponents worth taking seriously later. Three of them were built, namely the armored ships "A" (= DEUTSCHLAND"), "B" (= ADMIRAL SCHEER) and "C" (= ADMIRAL GRAF SPEE"). From ship to ship, improvements had been made which brought about increases every time to the limits of 10,000 tons (based on the type displacement) imposed by the Versailles Treaty, each time by several hundred tons. In the autumn of 1932, the discussion began at the top of the naval command as to how the armored ship "D" should appear, as the contract for its construction was to be given, according to the planning schedule, in the autumn of 1934. Admiral Raeder, at that time the Chief of Naval Operations, had already brought about an increase to 18,000 tons for the third armored ship and considered something similar for the new ship too. A few months after the discussion began, there was a change in command of the German Reich as Hitler was named to be Reich Chancellor. At this time the French had just laid the keel of their first postwar battleship, the DUNKERQUE, as the "answer" to the German armored ships, and this ship began to appear more and more clearly as their future adversary. High command positions in the German Navy thus took an anti-DUNKERQUE position and demanded a ship that was at least its equal.

Naturally Hitler agreed in principle to contracting for this fourth armored ship, but he

December 8, 1936: The launching. It is easy to see the black-painted section of the outer hull surface above the waterline to which the heavy side armor was later fastened. To the left of the GNEISENAU is the heavy cruiser "G", which was launched half a year later and christened with the name BLUCHER.

raised objections, mainly of a political nature, to increased armament — particularly to an increase in caliber. For that reason, Raeder ordered in June of 1933 that the design work for this new ship be brought to a conclusion as quickly as possible. It was to equal its predecessors in speed and primary armament but be more durable than them, which principally meant heavier armor. This meant a considerable increase in its displacement. The official design, finished toward the end of 1933, thus called for a new ship with the following characteristics:[1]

Type displacement	20,000 tons
Waterline/overall length	225/230 meters
Overall width	22.5 meters
Draught	8.5 meters
Powerplant/power	Turbines/125,000 HP
Top speed	29 knots
Armor	Waterline 220mm
	Citadel 50mm
	Upper deck 35mm
	Armor deck 80 mm (decreasing to 70 mm fore and aft), slopes 80mm
	Command post 300mm
Heavy artillery	Six 28 cm (possibly 8 in quadruple turrets)
Medium artillery	Eight 15-cm
Anti-aircraft guns	Eight 105mm plus 37- & 20mm Flak.
Torpedo tubes	Planned for the future

Despite all efforts, the hull could not be brought to a stop soon enough and struck against the nearby Hindenburg Embankment, which was pushed in for several meters, but did itself no great damage. The pictures show the hull just entering the water and, below, being taken in tow after striking and moved to the equipping pier.

A noteworthy feature of this design was the departure from the newly introduced motor drive. It was precisely this that had given the previous pocket battleships those characteristics that made them ideally suited to oceanic cruiser activity. Because the manufacturers needed several more years of development time to prepare motors with considerably greater performance, only steam turbines could be considered for use in the two new pocket battleships.

The contract for Armored Ship "D" was given to the Reich Naval Shipyard at Wilhelmshaven on January 25, 1934. There the keel was laid on February 14, 1934.

As of October 1933, the German Navy's plans included a fifth armored ship ("E"); it was to be built simultaneously with Armored Ship "D", as of April 1, 1934 (and not in 1937 as originally planned). Final permission was given on February 28, 1934, but the building contract — in advance, so to speak — had already been given on January 25, 1934; it went to the Deutsche Werke in Kiel, the former Imperial Shipyard. On February 14, 1934 — the same day as that of Armored Ship "D" — the keel was laid there too.

On June 27, 1934 there was a discussion between Hitler and Raeder in which the naval disagreements on the primary armament of the two new ships were discussed again. To be sure, there was agreement that these new ships, with their six 28-cm guns, would have no chance against the DUNKERQUE with its eight 33-cm guns. At this time, of course, Hitler could not be persuaded to allow an increase in caliber, but he did agree to increase the planned six 28-cm guns to nine. This permission led Raeder to call for a revision: Such an increase in the number of guns could be achieved only by adding one turret, and this condition made a completely new design necessary. This, though, caused a delay of twenty months. Early in July Raeder made his decision: On July 5, 1934 the work on the two newly begun pocket battleships was ordered halted, and a little later the slipways were cleared of the built-up material.

During the course of further research it was found that even with nine 28-cm guns it would be difficult to withstand an opponent like the DUNKERQUE. Hitler did grant a free hand in terms of calibers, but the naval leadership came to the conclusion that another revision would result in another delay of 16 to 22 months, and this was not wanted at all. Instead, the Navy made the suggestion of installing the planned primary armament of nine 28-cm guns but to rearm with a larger caliber at a later date; at first the 35-cm caliber was suggested, but one of 38-cm was finally agreed on.

The German-British fleet agreement accepted in June of 1935 then created the external conditions by which the restrictions of Versailles could be overcome. Directly after the agreement was accepted, the German government made the construction plans for its navy public, at the head of which stood "two armored ships of 26,000 tons with 28-cm guns" (the designation of "armored ship" was soon changed to "battleship"). The contracts signed with the two shipyards in January of 1934 remained in effect. Battleship "E" had its keel laid at the Deutsche Werke in Kiel on May 6, 1935 and was given construction number 235, just six weeks before its sister ship "D", the later SCHARNHORST. Twenty months later, on December 8, 1936, it was launched and christened with the name GNEISENAU, and on May 21, 1938 it could be commissioned for service, after a total building time of about three years.

[1] Data from Gröner, *Die deutschen Kriegsschiffe 1815-1945, Vol. I,* p.91.

THE POWERPLANT *

As desirable as motor drive would have been for these new ships, it had to be dispensed with in the end because a motor type was not yet available that was suitable for their size and their required speed. For that reason the decision had to be made to use steam turbine power, because only with it could the required high performance be achieved. High-pressure hot steam was an available new type of steam production. It had been used for some time in civilian facilities on land as well as in several civilian ships, and its utility had been proved thoroughly. In the course of the warship building continued after the governmental change of 1933, the decision was made for high-pressure hot-steam power and a number of new units were equipped with it; as of the spring of 1935 they were ready for service. Contrary to all expectations, though, their new-type power-

* Data in part from documents in the Witte legacy.

plants caused considerable displeasure on account of regularly recurring disturbances and shortcomings. Only through years of work, extending into the war, could the system be brought somewhat under control, but the problems were never completely eliminated. Here it was seen very clearly that this type of powerplant had been introduced too hastily and without years of systematic, step-by-step testing. For this class too there were problems and continuing difficulties with the powerplant, which could be overcome only with a lot of trouble.

The three-shaft main machine system consisted of three three-section turbine sets built by the Kiel Krupp-Germania Shipyard, with 44-ata turbine pressure and 470-degree steam temperature, each designed to produce 53,350 horsepower (for a total of 160,050 HP); they were the most powerful ever installed in German warships —even the turbines installed in the battleships **TIRPITZ** and **BISMARCK** could not equal them.

Power transmission took place via gear drive to each of the three three-bladed propellers, of 4.45-meter displacement. The primary running speed in the high-pressure stage was 6700 rpm, in the medium-pressure stage 3200 rom, and in the low-pressure stage 2700 rpm. These pressure stages were grouped around the drives, but the reverse high-pressure turbine was separate and the reverse low-pressure stage was in the low-pressure turbine, with a reverse power of 13,000 HP per turbine set.

The steam was produced in twelve Wagner high-pressure hot-steam boilers with natural water circulation, which were located in three boiler rooms in groups of four. The boiler pressure was 58 atü, the steam temperature 450 decrees Celsius. Each boiler had a heated surface of 425 square meters. The amount of steam produced, according to design statistics, was 55.7 t/h, the actual production ranged from 42 to a maximum of 54.5 t/h.

Along with these boilers there was another auxiliary boiler which was used only in harbor and produced up to 10 t/h of steam. The production of boiler-feed water from seawater was done by four freshwater production systems, one of which also provided washing and drinking water.

To produce all the ship's electric power there were five generator systems:
Two Diesel generators, each of 150 kilowatts, two Diesel generators of 300 kilowatts each, six turbine generators of 460 kilowatts each, two turbine generators of 230 kilowatts each, and one alternating-current generator off 200 kVA linked to a 230-kilowatt turbine generator. In all, 4120 kilowatts of power at 220 volts were produced.

The weight ratio per unit of the powerplant was stated at 17.5 kg/HP. The individual weights were as follows:

Turbines	970 tons
Boilers	1100 tons
Shafts and propellers	366 tons
Auxiliary machinery	80 tons
total	2516 tons

Over a measured mile the **GNEISENAU** produced 153,893 HP, attained a top speed of 30.70 knots and thus remained barely one knot slower than her sister ship **SCHARNHORST**.

Schematic drawing of the powerplant system:

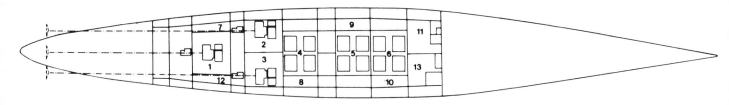

1. Turbine room 1
2. Turbine room 2
3. Turbine room 3
4. Boiler room 1
5. Boiler room 2
6. Boiler room 3
7. Generator 1
8. Generator 2
9. Generator 3
10. Generator 4
11. Generator 5
12. Electric machine room
13. Auxiliary boiler room

January 1938: The work of equipping is in full swing. Here the ship lies in the floating dock at its shipyard and is already covered with a first coat of paint.

This picture was taken in the spring of 1938: The equipping work is nearly finished, the time of commissioning is not far away. In the background is the school sailing ship GORCH FOCK.

April 1938: Underway for the first time, but not completely equipped. Still lacking are, among other things, the range-finder covers, the anti-aircraft command post and the cranes. This is a so-called "factory cruise", carried out exclusively by shipyard personnel.

PROTECTIVE ARMOR

In designing this class, the German Navy stuck to its proved principle of giving the "durability" factor the absolute priority over all other fighting values. This was favored further through the politically expedient decision against a higher caliber for the heavy artillery. The weight thus saved could thus be used to increase the durability.

In these ships the newly developed armoring materials "Wotan hart" ("Wh") and "Wotan weich" ("Ww") were used for the first time, and used, in fact, in place of the previously used shipbuilding steel in the areas of outer hull and horizontal protection. This offered the possibility of extending the protection considerably over the entire ship. Both materials were special alloys, which replaced the KNC armor (of the same composition as KC armor but not cemented [1] and the nickel armor used up to the "K"-class cruisers; while neither KNC nor nickel armor could be welded, both "Wh" and "Ww" could be welded very well with special electrodes. The "Wh" and "Ww" material was used in thicknesses from 10 to 150mm. [2]

With a thickness of 350mm, the side armor, about 5 meters wide, was strong enough to withstand at least the 33-cm shells of the DUNKERQUE. A definite weak point was the citadel armor, which extended from the upper edge of the side armor up to the upper deck and had been made too thin. The total thickness of the horizontal armor could be regarded as sufficient at the time it was planned. The upper deck — which was also the main deck — was given less thick armor, for reasons of stability, than the actual armor deck two levels below it.

This was done on the principle that striking shells or bombs would be "braked" in terms of penetrating potential by the (more lightly) armored upper deck and forced to detonate against the armor deck; the destruction of the area between the armor and upper decks was therefore accepted because it was used mainly for the crew's quarters and was of little importance to the ship's fighting power. This principle proved itself thoroughly. For example, the GNEISENAU took three bomb hits at Brest, all of which detonated against the armor deck after breaking through the upper deck. Only as bomb weights increased did it become clear that the horizontal armor had, in the end, been made too thin. This became especially clear in February of 1942, when a 454-kilogram armor-piercing bomb hit the forward part of the GNEISENAU and had a catastrophic effect.

The underwater protection was planned to withstand torpedo and mine hits with charges of up to 250 kilograms. It consisted of a torpedo bulkhead running parallel to the outer hull, inclined ten degrees from the vertical and made of "Ww" material. Its distance from the outer

---

[1] KC armor meant "Krupp Cemented."
[2] "Wh" tear resistance 85 to 95 kg/cu.mm, flexibility 20%, stretching limit 50 to 55 kg/sq.mm, "Ww" tear resistance 65 to 75 kg/sq.mm, flexibility 25%, stretching limit 38 to 40 kg/sq.mm (according to Marineoberbaurat Dipl.Ing. K.K. Többicke: *Die Panzerung der deutschen Kriegsschiffe von 1919 bis 1945*, unprinted manuscript of 1951-52).

The installation of the "Anton" turret: A floating crane is installing the turning circle with the mantelet frame. Inside the support cylinder already built into the ship's hull the swinging bearing can be seen, the balls of which are the size of children's heads.

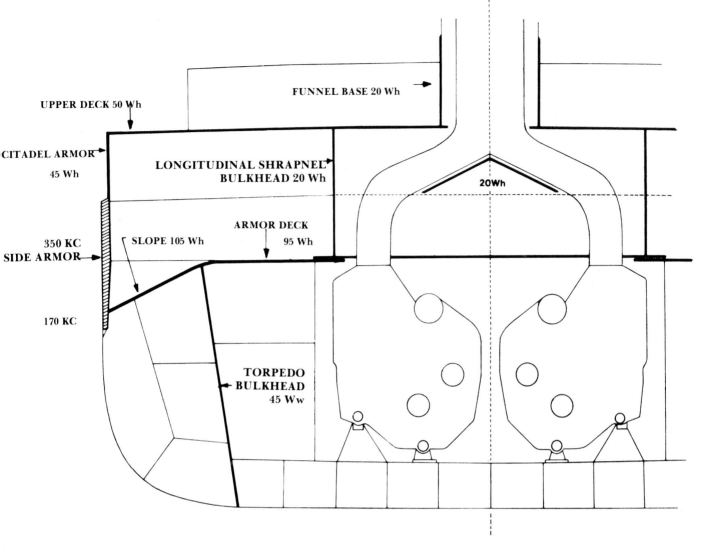

UPPER DECK 50 Wh

CITADEL ARMOR
45 Wh

FUNNEL BASE 20 Wh

LONGITUDINAL SHRAPNEL
BULKHEAD 20 Wh

20Wh

350 KC
SIDE ARMOR

SLOPE 105 Wh

ARMOR DECK
95 Wh

170 KC

TORPEDO
BULKHEAD
45 Ww

Cross-section amidships, with armor. The armor material and its thickness in millimeters are indicated. Wh = Wotan hart (hard), Ww = Wotan weich (soft), KC = Krupp Cementiert (cemented).

Taken during equipping: a look at the ''Anton'' and ''Bruno'' turrets and the bridge superstructure.

This picture, taken in June of 1938, shows the battleship running the measured mile. The thick clouds of smoke indicate that all boilers are in use.

skin was about 4.5 meters in the middle. The space between the torpedo bulkhead and the outer skin was also divided in the middle by another, thinner longitudinal bulkhead. This design proved itself completely. An example was provided by the air torpedo that hit the GNEISENAU in Brest; it tore the outer skin open but did not even bend the torpedo bulkhead.

The ship's bottom was not particularly protected against mines. The material thicknesses of joints and plating simply met the requirements for the ship's rigidity, but the watertight division and strengthening of the double bottom was formed particularly carefully to make up for it. This type of bottom protection of large warships was sufficient until into 1942, for example during the Channel breakthrough, where both the GNEISENAU and the SCHARNHORST came away with mine damage.

The individual armor thicknesses were [3]:
Side armor (between Ribs 32 and 207): 350mm, thinner below (tapered) to 170mm; at the bow 150mm "Wh" (tapered to 70mm) and at the stern 200mm "Wh" (tapered to 170mm).
Armor bulkheads: 150 to 200mm.
Citadel armor (in same form as side armor): 45mm, aft 35mm, forward 20mm.
Longitudinal shrapnel bulkhead in citadel area: 20mm "Wh."
Upper deck: 50mm "Wh."
Armor deck: 80 to 95mm "Wh" with slopes 105-110mm "Wh."
Torpedo bulkhead: 45mm "Wh."
Forward command post: Sides 350mm, roof 200mm, shaft 220mm.
After command post: Sides 100mm, roof 50mm, shaft 100mm.
Range finder covers on command posts: 100mm.
Artillery command post (foretop): 60mm, roof 20mm, range finder cover 20mm.
Anti-aircraft command posts: 14mm.
28-cm turrets: front 360mm, sides 180mm, back 350mm, roof 180mm, barbettes 350mm.
15-cm turrets: front 140mm, sides 50mm, back 50mm, roof 50mm, barbettes 150mm.
15-cm single guns: front 25mm.
105mm anti-aircraft guns: front 20mm.

The total weight of the armor (without turning armor) added up to 14,245 tons = ca. 40% of the design displacement, of which 6580 tons amounted to KC armor, as follows:

Barbettes for heavy artillery	2469 tons
Barbettes for medium artillery	467 tons
Side armor	3440 tons
Armored bulkheads	204 tons
	6580 tons

The ship was divided into 21 watertight compartments, and a double bottom stretched along some 79% of the ship's length. The side height measured 14 meters. Every 55.1 tons of added weight meant an increase of 10mm in draught.

[3] All KC material, unless otherwise stated.

10

THE ARMAMENT

The armament of the battleship GNEISENAU was composed of heavy artillery (SA), medium artillery (MA) and anti-aircraft artillery.

The SA consisted of nine 28-cm quick-loading cannons (S.K.) L/54.5 C/34 in C/34 rotating mantelets, mounted in three triple turrets. The turrets were the same as those used in pocket battleships of the DEUTSCHLAND class, but the armor was thickened appropriately. The guns were made to a new, high-performance design. The barrels weighed 52,250 kg.

BALLISTIC PERFORMANCE *

Shot range	Barrel elevation	Impact angle	Shot speed m/sec
5,000	2.0 degrees	2.5 degrees	766
10,000	4.3 degrees	5.7 degrees	652
15,000	7.4 degrees	10.3 degrees	556
20,000	11.3 degrees	25.7 degrees	436
25,000	16.2 degrees	25.7 degrees	436
30,000	22.0 degrees	35.3 degrees	418
35,000	29.2 degrees	44.0 degrees	428
40,000	38.2 degrees	52.0 degrees	460

* According to Campbell, *Naval Weapons of World War II*

The first photograph of the GNEISENAU released to the daily and technical press by the Naval High Command was published on the occasion of her commissioning for service; it was taken in the first days of May 1938 and shows the ship not yet completely equipped.

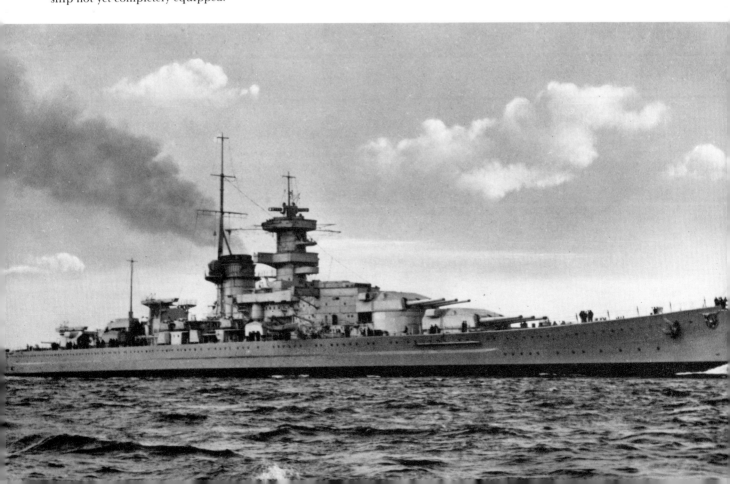

The front 28-cm triple turrets, both swung to port. The "Bruno" turret as far as it will go. At the lower edge of the photo is the forward port boat boom; here it has been swung out and used to fasten the ship's launched boats and facilitate movement between the boats and the ship.

The ammunition supply amounted to 150 rounds per gun. This was divided, in its totality, into 450 armor-penetrating shells, 450 explosive shells with impact fuses and 450 explosive shells with nose fuses.

The guns — their barrel bores measuring 283mm and their distance from each other (measured from inner axis to inner axis) 2.75 meters — had a maximum range of 398 hm at a barrel elevation of 40 degrees. The lifetime of a barrel was calculated at 300 rounds. The barrel recoil measured 1.20 meters. The cadence was 3.75 rounds per minute, meaning they could be fired every 17 seconds. The movable part of the turret weighed 750 tons, its barbettes had an interior diameter of 10.20 meters. The aiming speed was about 7.2 degrees per second in traverse and 8 degrees per second in elevation.

The elevation arc extended from -8 degrees (turret raised 9 degrees) to +40 degrees. The guns could be coupled together or handled separately. The turret crew numbered 75 men. In every turret was a range finder with a 10.50-meter base; the ends of the base were inside hoods that curved out from the sides of the turret.

The guns fired explosive shells with nose fuses, explosive shells with impact fuses, and armor-piercing shells. The first type weighed 315 kg (including an explosive charge of 21.8 kg), those with impact fuses weighed 330 kg (16-kg explosive charge), and the armor-piercing shells also weighed 330 kg but had an explosive charge of only 6.6 kg. The propellant charge was divided between two cartridges, a 44-kg preliminary and a 127-kg main cartridge.

Painting the "Anton" turret. For this purpose the gun barrels are lowered to their lowest position, and the leather covers that sealed the aiming openings on the turret front have been removed. These openings were the most sensitive parts of the turret; it was never possible to make them completely watertight. In heavy seas the front turrets often had to be swung far enough so the breaking seas struck their sidewalls.

After being commissioned — the battle flag flying on the stern flagpole shows that this has taken place — floating cranes load the last items aboard at the shipyard. On the stern is the national eagle that was then obligatory for all German warships. In the background the pocket battleship ADMIRAL GRAF SPEE can be seen.

In the summer of 1938 tests were made with various single-engine seaplanes that could be catapult-launched, such as the one-and-a-half-wing Heinkel He 114 and the Arado Ar 95 and Focke-Wulf Fw 62 biplanes. The picture shows an He 114 being lifted aboard by the port airplane crane. The rolled-up Hein'sche Landing Sail, which was dispensed with in 1939, can be seen on the upper deck. On the rear catapult is an Fw 62 V1.

In September of 1938 the decision was made that Kiel would be the main port of the GNEISENAU, after it had taken over the role of fleet flagship from the pocket battleship ADMIRAL GRAF SPEE. During the war the GNEISENAU could often be seen as she is here, made fast to Buoy A 11 in Kiel Harbor.

This picture taken in June of 1938 shows the beginning of training. Apparently the crew is learning how the ship functions, as indicated by the various traverse and elevation positions of the guns and catapult. The rear starboard anti-aircraft command post is still lacking.

The shell left the barrel at an initial velocity (Vo) of 890 meters per second. The penetrating power of the armor-piercing shell was:

Range	Penetrated Side	Deck Armor
hm	Armor mm	Width mm
790	460	19
1510	355	41
1828	291	48

Considered from the start but never actually prepared for was a later rearmament with six 38-cm guns in three double turrets. The diameter of the barbettes would not have needed to be expanded for the purpose; just by chance, it appears, this was the same for the 38-cm double as for the 28-cm triple turret. According to peacetime planning, this rearmament was to have been done in the winter of 1940-41, thus shortly after the battleship BISMARCK was commissioned for service.

The medium artillery consisted of twelve 15-cm L/55 C/28 guns, but only two thirds of the guns could be mounted on C/34 turning mantelets in double turrets. For lack of space, the other four had to be placed in C/28 central-pivot mantelets with simple shields. The weight of the swinging part of a 15-cm twin turret was 114 tons. Its barbette had a diameter of 4.80 meters. The arc of elevation extended from -10 to +40 degrees, while that of the 15-cm single guns was only from -10 to +35 degrees. The shot ranges reached a maximum of 230 hm at 40-

The maiden voyage of the GNEISENAU ran from June 30 to July 8, 1938; without stopping at a harbor, she covered about 4500 nautical miles. On the return trip she passed the Pentland Firth, difficult to master navigationally, between the northern point of Great Britain and the Orkneys. This picture was obviously taken there from aft, looking forward.

On July 22, 1938 Hitler visited the
Navy, including going aboard the
GNEISENAU. On this occasion
the "Führer's flag" was flown at
the maintop for the duration of his
time on board. Here —obviously
for Hitler to watch — a cutter race
is taking place.

During a period spent in the shipyard, lasting from October to December of 1938, the GNEISENAU was fitted with a
more advantageous "Atlantic bow" as well as a diagonal cap on the funnel. These modifications were intended to
improve seaworthiness and keep the tower mast-bridge complex free of smoke. A close look suggests that the previously
used smokestack braces are missing; they are actually present as before, but covered by the funnel cap. In the spring of
1939 this design was changed again, with a narrower funnel cap, so that the braces were again outside it.

August 22, 1938 was a special day for the Navy: On the occasion of the state visit of Admiral Nikolaus Horthy von
Nagybanya, the regent of the Reich's ally Hungary at that time, the greatest fleet parade since World War I took place
in Kiel Bay — and remained the only one of its kind. Since from the union with Austria on the Navy was responsible
for preserving the traditions of the former Imperial and Royal Navy, the flag of this former navy, whose last
commander was Admiral Horthy, is flying from the maintop. The crew of the GNEISENAU has taken parade position
(men in white, petty officers without sword-knot in blue and white, officers and petty officers with sword-knot — the
officers at the stern — in blue). The flag of the fleet chief flies from the foretop.

degree barrel elevation (twin turret) and 220 hm at 35-degree elevation (single gun). A cadence of 8 rounds per minute was attainable. Explosive shells weighing 45.3 kg left the barrel with a Vo of 875 m/sec. The lifetime of a barrel was calculated at 1000 rounds. The ammunition supply of the total medium artillery added up to 1600 rounds (800 explosive shells each with nose and impact fuses); in wartime, 240 tracer shells were added.

The heavy anti-aircraft guns were especially numerous, numbering fourteen. The 105mm Flak L/65 C/33 was used in turning (double) C/31 mantelets. These had a weight of 27,805 kg and an elevation arc from -8 to +80 degrees. The aiming speed was 8 degrees per second for traverse and 10 degrees per second for elevation. The maximum attainable rate of fire was 18 rounds per minute. The maximum range was 177 hm; at 80-degree elevation the highest altitude was 12,500 meters. The guns fired 15.1-kg uniform ammunition; the initial velocity of the shell was 900 m/sec. The total supply of ammunition numbered 6020 rounds, making 830 rounds per double mantelet (explosive shells), with 420 tracer cartridges also available.

The light-caliber anti-aircraft weapons were sixteen 37mm Flak L/83 C/30 guns (maximum range 830 km at 37.5-degree elevation, altitude 6800 meters at 85-degree elevation, initial velocity 1000 m/sec, weight of the cartridge 0.748 kg, cadence theoretically up to 80 rounds per minute, in practice only about 30 rounds per minute). 32,000 explosive shells of this caliber were carried, making 4000 per double mantelet.

There were also ten single 20mm FlaMG C/30 guns on C/30 socket mantelets (cadence in practice approximately 120 rounds per minute), which were replaced in January of 1941 by 20mm FlaMG C-38 (cadence in practice 220 rounds per minute).

During the war the light anti-aircraft weapons were increased. On January 14, 1941 the GNEISENAU was equipped with quadruple 20mm anti-aircraft guns on a high platform ("stork's nest") behind the funnel (during the hangar installation at Brest, though, it was removed again). In the same year, three more quadruple 20mm guns were installed, one on top of the "Bruno" turret, one on the ring platform around the funnel and one on the after superstructure, making a total of 22 20mm guns. The total ammunition supply added up to 20,000 explosive cartridges.

According to the original plans, a torpedo weapon was not included. But because of the experience gained in action against merchant shipping in the Atlantic, two triple sets of 53, 30mm torpedo tubes, taken from the light cruiser LEIPZIG, were installed at Brest in the summer of 1941. The torpedo fire control system used there, though, was not taken over. Storage was provided on board for 18 "G 7a" torpedoes (430-kg charge, speed/range knots/miles 30/15,000, 40/5000, 45/4500).

Fire control: In addition to the 10.50-meter range finders built into the "Bruno" and "Cäsar" turrets [1], there were three other large range finders: the tower mast and the after command post each had an armored turning cover with a 105mm base, and there was another, with a 6-meter base, on the forward command post. For the anti-aircraft guns there were four triaxially stabilized SL-6 Flak fire control posts, each with a 4-meter base; these posts could be recognized by their covers, shaped like segments of a sphere, and were known in naval slang as

[1] The 10.50-meter range finder in the "Anton" turret was removed, along with its covers, at the beginning of 1942, and the openings in the turret were sealed, because the latter had been a constant source of sea water that entered the turret and affected its functioning reliability.

Also taken on August 22, 1938: The GNEISENAU — here lying at her mooring buoy in Kiel and flying flags over her tops — fires a salute for the Hungarian guest of honor. A part of the crew has taken up parade position.

The new prow form certainly improved the ship's seaworthiness, but the relatively low-lying bow anchor proved to be the cause of an unpleasant buildup of spray at higher speeds. For that reason, the hawseholes were welded shut in the spring of 1939 and so-called bowed hawseholes were made on the upper deck for the bow anchors — of which there were only two from now on; this decreased the spray buildup to some extent. Here the GNEISENAU is seen in the spring of 1939 with the new type of hawseholes.

"wobbly pots." In addition, there was a smaller open (i.e., not protected) range finder on the lower forward platform of the tower mast. Since the autumn of 1939 there was an FuMO 22 radar device on the turning cover of the foretop, replaced in the summer of 1941 by an FuMO 27. At the beginning of 1942 a radar antenna (presumably FuMO 27) was also installed on the after turning cover.

The airplanes carried on board also counted among the ship's weapons. For them there were two compressed-air catapults, each 14 meters long. One of them was amidships, set on a catapult tower barely 8 meters high and rotating 360 degrees. A hangar was planned from the beginning, but it was only built in the summer of 1938 and disappeared again toward the end of 1939, as it — presumably because of its too-small storage space — did not seem satisfactory. Four airplanes were intended to be carried on board, two in the hangar and one on each of the catapults. As of the end of 1939, a hangar was dispensed with altogether, and in practice there was usually just a single plane on board; only at Brest was a newly designed hangar built.

The second catapult was built on top of the "Cäsar" turret and could turn only with it. Aft of it on the port side was a crane which, when not in use, could be dismantled and lain on the deck. With this crane — by a very laborious process — a plane could be lifted off the forward catapult (or onto it); the plane, having been lifted by the port airplane crane, had to be taken up, while in the air, by this crane. Since this catapult, on account of its heavy weight, made rotating the turret difficult and otherwise proved to be more bother than it was worth, it was removed from the ship in February of 1940. Even before that, the Hein'sche Landing Sail kept on the port side had been removed, as its use proved to be too laborious and time-consuming under wartime conditions.

The GNEISENAU originally carried two experimental Arado 95 seaplanes, but tests were also made with Heinkel 114 and Focke-Wulf 62 planes. From 1939 on Arado 196 planes were used.

OTHER EQUIPMENT

There were five triaxially stabilized floodlights on board, each of 1.60-meter diameter. The two after ones (removed in 1942) were mounted on lifting pedestals. Lifting tackle included two airplane and two boat cranes, plus the airplane moving crane, which was removed in 1940. Boats included one motor pinnace, three tenders, two motor jollyboats, three cutters, officially ten boats in all. At first there were three bow anchors (one at starboard, two at port), as of 1939 only two, plus a rear anchor carried in a port-side hawsehole. The ship also possessed a mine-protection system (MES cable loop on the upper edge of the side armor). Two parallel spade rudders were set outside the wash of the side propellers.

17

TECHNICAL DATA[1]

Displacement, empty ship:	30,676 tons
Type displacement:	26,000 tons planned, 32,082 tons actual
Design displacement:	35,398 tons
Action displacement:	38,434 tons
Length at design waterline:	226.00 meters
Length overall:	229.80/234.90 meters[2]
Width at design waterline:	30.00 meters
Width overall:	30.00 meters
Draught at design displacement:	8.23 meters
Draught at action displacement:	9.91 meters

Speed according to design[3]	Powerplant performance	Revolutions Attained
Highest attained HP	Knots of Speed	RPM
160,050	265	28.0
151,893	280	30.7

Capacities[4]		
	Heating oil	5360 cubic meters[5]
	Fuel oil	174 " "
	Cooking water	563 " "
	Washing water	354 " "
	Drinking water	149 " "

Range:	Expected: 8200 nautical miles at 19 knots
	Attained: 6200 " " " 19 "

Crew in wartime: 1669 men

Construction cost: 146,174,000 Reichsmark

Measurements taken at design displacement[6]: Freeboard forward/amidships: 8.30/4.80 meters. L/B ratio (length to width) 7.53, B/T (width to depth) 3.26, L/H (length to height) 16.17. Degree of displacement: 0.55. Cylinder coefficient 0.57. Degree of main rib 0.96, Degree of design waterline 0.66.

---

[1] According to documents in the Witte Legacy.
[2] Before/after the prow was rebuilt.
[3] According to Garzke, Dulin: *Battleships – Axis and Neutral Battleships in World War II*, p. 201.
[4] According to Kähler, *Schlachtschiff GNEISENAU* (Series: Men-Ships-Fates), pp. 31 ff.
[5] With maximum utilization of all bunker space, up to ca. 6000 square meters.
[6] According to Hadeler, *Kriegsschiffbau*, Vol. I, pp. 328 ff.

Taken in June of 1939: The GNEISENAU making steam while lying at the mooring buoy in Kiel Harbor. The boat booms are already lashed down; only the gangway is still deployed.

WEIGHT-GROUP SUMMARIES [1]

Weight group	Weight (tons)	Percentage (approx.)
Ship's body	8,316	23.5
Armor (not rotating)	14,245	40.2
Main machines (& equipment)	2,680	7.5
Auxiliary machines	1,114	3.1
Artillery (+ turning armor)	3,935	11.1
Aircraft equipment	90	0.2
Blockade weapons	8	0.0
General equipment	259	
Nautical instruments	9	0.8
Tackle	30	
Displacement of empty ship	**30,686**	**86.6**
Ammunition for artillery	1,195	3.3
Ammunition for blockade weapons	1	0.0
Materials for consumption	111	0.3
Crew and effects	201	0.6
Provisions	151	0.5
Drinking water	117	0.3
Washing water	140	0.4
Type displacement	**32,604**	**91.8**
Cooking water	285	0.9
Heating oil	2.407	6.8
Fuel oil	72	
Lubricating oil	25	0.3
Aircraft fuel	13	
Design displacement	**35,406**	**100.0**
Cooking water	286	
Heating oil	2,424	
Fuel oil	72	
Lubricating oil	25	
Aircraft fuel	13	
Fresh water reserve	217	
Action displacement	**38,443**	

[1] According to documents in the Witte legacy.

A six-week training cruse taken in the summer of 1939 took the GNEISENAU into the mid-Atlantic and allowed the crew a short stop at Las Palmas, in the Canary Islands.

In 1939 the Arado Ar 196 reconnaissance plane was introduced. The GNEISENAU was equipped with them Here an Ar 196 sits on the forward catapult, with the swiveling mount of the starboard aircraft crane at the lower right.

Kiel Harbor, August 1939: Peacetime routine still prevails on board. The forward boat boom and the gangway are deployed, the tenders have tied on in the lee.

All the large units of the Navy bore coats of arms at the bow that were closely related to their names. The GNEISENAU bore the family arms of the Prussian Field Marshal Count Neidhart von Gneisenau. Soon after the war began, the coat of arms was removed from the ship and stored on land. This picture was taken in Kiel Harbor in the summer of 1939.

The use of the second aircraft catapult, mounted on the top of the "Cäsar" turret, involved problems. One was that it required the combined use of the actual aircraft crane with the shifting crane installed farther aft and seen here raised.

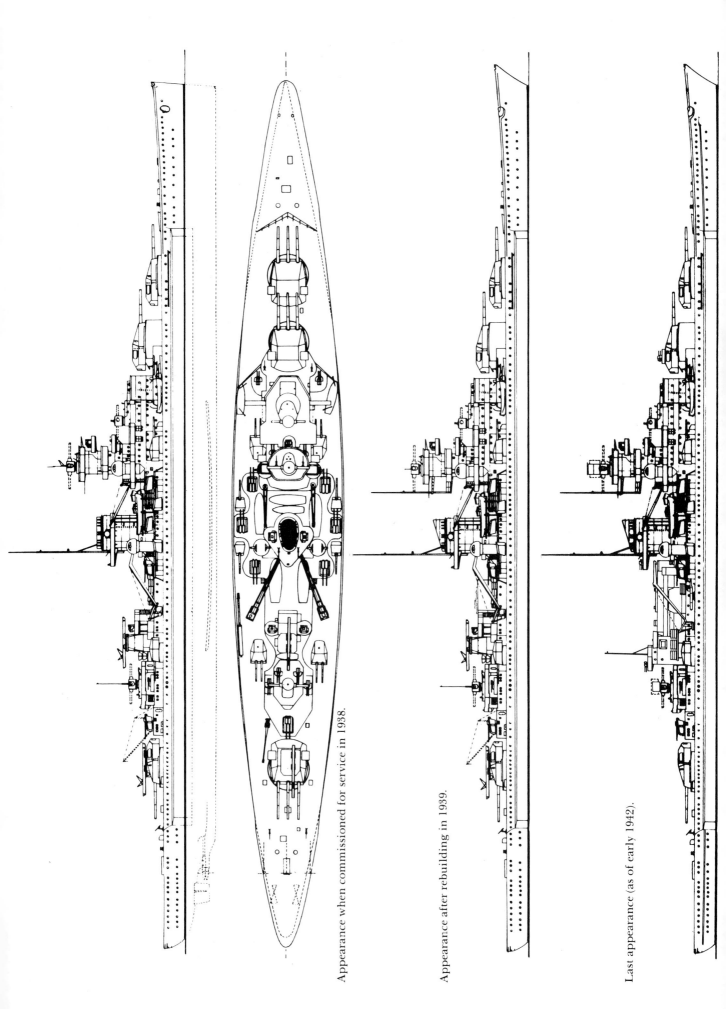

Appearance when commissioned for service in 1938.

Appearance after rebuilding in 1939.

Last appearance (as of early 1942).

After running the measured mile in the Baltic Sea off Neukrug (Kurische Nehrung) and then completing caliber firing, the GNEISENAU put in to the very iced-up inner firth at Kiel, where she took up her mooring place below the Hotel "Bellevue." From the next day on, traffic between her and the shore moved only on wooden planking laid over the ice. A few days later it was possible to move the ship through the thick ice into the Holtenau Lock. This picture, taken at that time, shows the MES cable loop right above the heavy side armor.

As fleet operations began, the crews of the ships involved were called aft where they were briefed — usually by their commanders — on the extent and purposes of the operations. This picture was taken in February 1940 just after they put out on Operation "Nordmark." In the wake of the GNEISENAU are two destroyers. At the left edge of the picture is the rear catapult installed on top of the "Cäsar" turret, here carrying an Ar 196 ready to take off; to the right of it is the servicing platform. The catapult was removed right after the ship returned from this operation.

The GNEISENAU shortly after putting in to Wilhelmshaven after completing Operation "Nordmark." Since the spring she bore a high rod mast mounted behind the tower mast in place of the short FT rod on top of the foretop turning cover. The antenna of the radar navigation gear, installed in November 1939, is seen on the turning cover.

In extremely low temperatures, a sheet of ice quickly spread over the ship and caused considerable danger. The gun turrets had to be turned time after time to prevent icing of the traverse and elevation aiming gear. This picture of the GNEISENAU was taken in February 1940 during Operation "Nordmark." At the top of the picture is the admiral's bridge, which has been enclosed.

The damage done by a mine in the mouth of the Elbe on May 5, 1940 was not excessively great. Repairs took only a short time, and two weeks later the ship could get underway again. This picture was taken in May 1940 in the floating dock of the Deutsche Werke at Kiel. The port and middle propellers can be seen clearly here.

A boat could have floated easily through the hole torn in the bow by a torpedo from the British U-boat CLYDE on June 20, 1940. The MES cable loop above the hole is easy to see.

After makeshift repairs were made in Trondheim, the GNEISENAU set off for home for permanent repairs and put in to Kiel on July 26, 1940, in good shape.

This is how the bow looked after the ship was docked" Over the huge hole one can see the covering at waterlineim. The picture was taken on July 31, 1940.

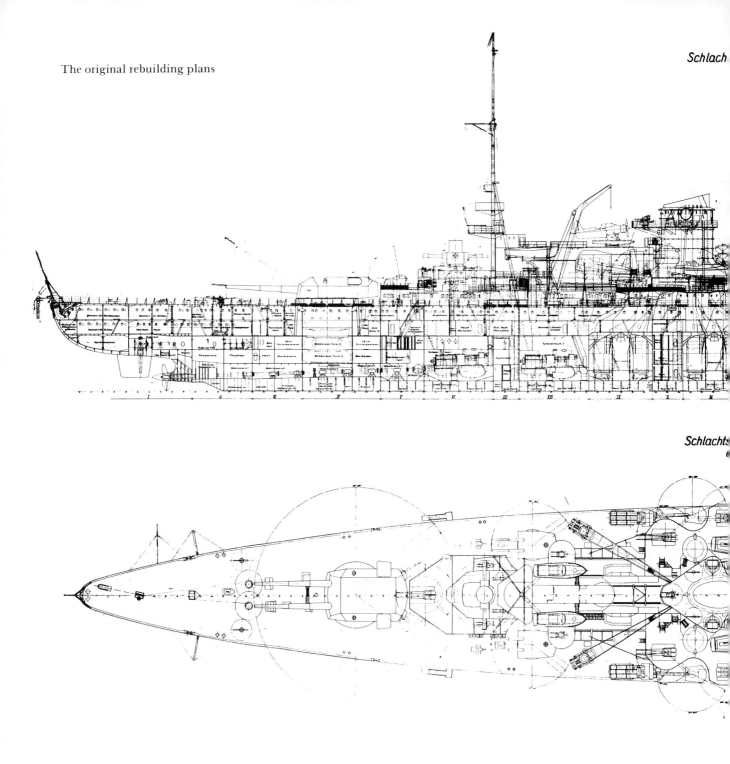

Meeting U 124 in the mid-Atlantic in the best of weather and an almost mirrorlike sea.

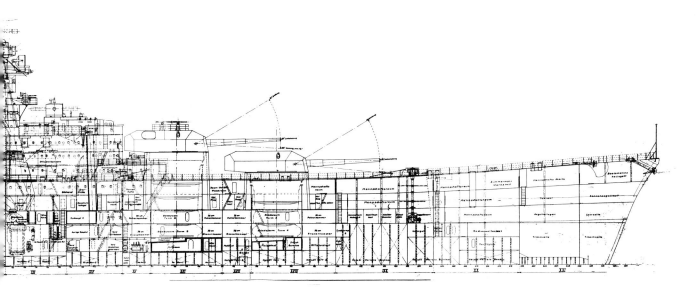

" K235/N4

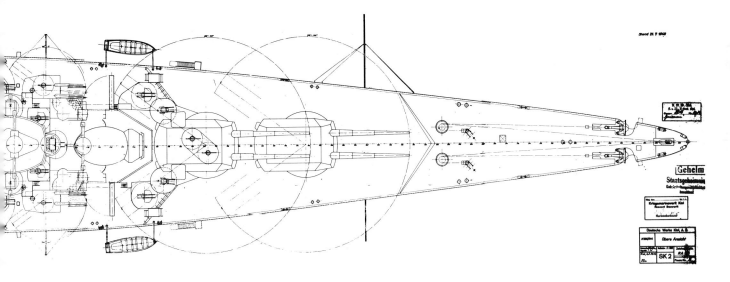

From this perspective the broken prow is visible. Below is the bow bulge with the opening for the "S" device.

Only in the dock could the deep tears made by the torpedo, some of them reaching almost to the keel, be seen.

The evening of June 7, 1940 — the group composed of the battleships GNEISENAU and SCHARNHORST, the heavy cruiser ADMIRAL HIPPER and four destroyers has stopped for a meeting of chief and command on the GNEISENAU in order to decide on the continuation of Operation "Juno." The group lay on the open sea in broad daylight for two hours — a year later that would no longer have been possible.

The picture was taken from the afterdeck of the cruiser ADMIRAL HIPPER; lying diagonally behind is the GNEISENAU, aft of it is the SCHARNHORST.

The pennants on the masts tell of the success of Operation "Berlin"; a machine overhaul lasting several weeks was scheduled for the GNEISENAU in Brest at that time, after which — in about the second half of April — she was to put out into the Atlantic and meet the battleship BISMARCK. Here the GNEISENAU is seen putting in to Brest.

A view forward from aft on the port side deck. In the foreground is the after port 37mm double anti-aircraft gun, over it the airplane catapult, and in the background the platform ring around the funnel.

Right after putting in to Brest on March 22, 1941, the crews of the sunk enemy ships were disembarked. Here they take positions in front of the ship to be sent to a prisoner-of-war camp after roll call.

On April 6, 1941 all plans were nullified: While the GNEISENAU waited to be docked, a British airplane scored an air torpedo hit that caused considerable damage aft. After the ship was docked, British planes scored four bomb hits four days later, which caused further heavy damage. Here one sees the just-docked GNEISENAU amidships.

Soon after the docking, a group of Japanese naval officers located in the German area had the chance to view the GNEISENAU. Here they stand before the after port 15-cm turret.

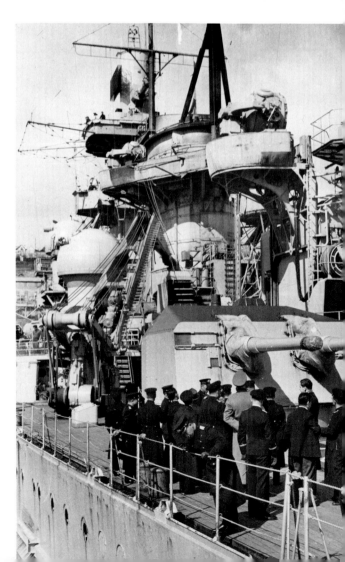

This gangway, guarded by a sentry with steel helmet and rifle, was the only connection between the ship and land during docking. Behind the funnel, the high platform with the 20mm quadruple anti-aircraft guns can be seen. The FT rod has been removed from the after range-finder cover; sandbags have been stacked under it as additional shrapnel protection.

Not long after docking an attempt was made to make the ship hard for the enemy to spot by using camouflage nets. Here again is a view from aft during the camouflaging work. In the foreground is the airplane catapult, and behind it is the "stork's nest" with the 20mm quadruple anti-aircraft guns.

The GNEISENAU while docked at Brest, seen from ahead, here without camouflage nets.

THE NEW AIRCRAFT SYSTEM

In the autumn of 1941 a new aircraft system was installed at Brest. This had been advocated on the basis of experience during Atlantic service and was to include not only a greater number of airplanes but also better hangar and service facilities. In place of the old catapult, a new hangar, some 27 meters long, 7 meters high and 6 meters wide, was built, inside which a 14-meter catapult was built. This could be turned 360 degrees, for which a sliding door on each side had to be opened (in the following order: rear door aft, middle door forward past forward door). This provided an opening somewhat over 13 meters long and barely 6 meters at its greatest height. Thus the airplane could be launched out of its hangar. A second plane could be housed in the rear part of the hangar, a third on the roof, in each case with its wings removed and shored along its fuselage. To be ready for launching, the catapult had to be swung into crosswise position; only then could the wings be mounted. The process had to be done in opposite order when the plane was brought in. It was not possible to open the hangar roof. Except for a few test takeoffs, this new system never was used.

The drawings:
1. Hangar (side view), closed by three-piece sliding door. A third Ar 196 is shown on the hangar roof. 2. Opened hangar (side view) with Ar 196 placed on the catapult and second Ar 196 in the rear section. 3. Hangar (from above) with Ar 196 ready for takeoff and second Ar 196. 4. Hangar (cross-section) with Ar 196 placed on the catapult.
The arrows show the directions in which the doors slide.

A look at the docked GNEISENAU, seen from a crane.

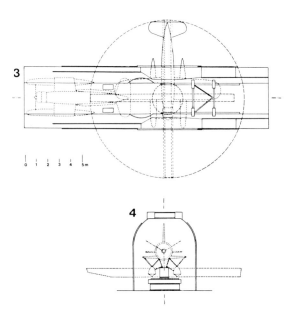

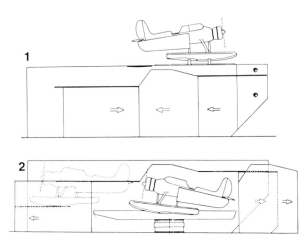

The new hangar. The numbers indicate: 1 = side view (port), 2 = side view (port) with sliding doors open, 3 = top view with catapult's rotating circle, 4 = cross-section. The arrows show the directions in which the doors are pushed.

Early in 1942 the GNEISENAU was fitted with the long-requested torpedo tubes; these were located amidships on the side decks. This picture shows the first torpedo-firing practice, which was done from the pier in Brest. The new hangar can also be seen, as can the radar position with antenna atop the after range-finder cover.

The GNEISENAU on January 26, 1942, before putting out to take part in Operation "Cerberus." Here the new hangar can be seen in its full extent. The catapult has been placed in it, so that it is possible to launch the airplane directly from the hangar. In it there is room for two Ar 196 planes (one of which sets on the catapult ready for takeoff), while a third Ar 196 could be kept on the roof of the hangar. The new mainmast that had already arrived at Brest was to be built against the after edge of the hangar, but there was no time to install it.

THE LIFE STORY OF THE BATTLESHIP GNEISENAU

May 6, 1935:	Keel laid at Deutsche Werke in Kiel.
December 8, 1936:	Launching.
May 21, 1938:	Commissioned for service.
June 30-July 8, 1938:	Maiden voyage to northern seas with side trip to northeastern Atlantic.
August 22, 1938:	Participated in fleet parade in Kiel Bight for state visit of Hungarian regent Admiral Nikolaus Horthy von Nagybanya.
October-December 1938:	Completion and rebuilding at Deutsche Werke in Kiel (prow, funnel cap, tower mast).
June-July 1939:	Six-week training cruise to mid-Atlantic, with frequent firing drill and supplying at sea; July 1-2, stop at Las Palmas, Canary Islands.
October 7-9, 1939:	Advance to latitude of south Norwegian coast along with cruiser KOLN and nine destroyers. No enemy contact.
November 21-27, 1939:	Advance with sister ship SCHARNHORST to waters south of Iceland, sank British auxiliary cruiser RAWALPINDI on November 23.
February 17-20, 1940:	Operation "Nordmark": advance with sister ship SCHARNHORST, heavy cruiser ADMIRAL HIPPER and nine destroyers to latitude of Shetland Islands and southern Norway. No enemy contact.
April 7-12, 1940:	Participation in Operation "Weserübung" (occupation of Norway and Denmark) by securing the units cruising to Narvik and Trondheim; April 8, combat with British battle cruiser RENOWN, received three hits, one serious, in foretop.
May 5, 1940:	During cruise in Baltic Sea, serious damage from remote-control mine.
June 4-July 26, 1940:	Operation "Juno": advance to relieve German troops under pressure in Norway along with sister ship SCHARNHORST, cruiser ADMIRAL HIPPER and four destroyers, ran into hitherto unknown British transfer action from Norway. Sank British carrier GLORIOUS and cruisers ARDENT and ACASTA on June 8, then put in to Trondheim. Left there June 20 and advanced to Line Island, Faroes, Orkneys, took torpedo hit in bow from British U-boat CLYDE; returned to Trondheim for makeshift repairs; July 25, headed home for repairs.
July 26-November 14, 1940:	Docked and repaired at Deutsche Werke, Kiel.
December 28, 1940:	Put out with SCHARNHORST for breakthrough into Atlantic to wage war against British merchant shipping; got into heavy storm, operation broken off because of considerable damage.
January 2, 1941:	Put in to Gotenhafen for repair of sea damage.
January 22, 1941:	Put out with SCHARNHORST for Operation "Berlin"; February 3-4, breakthrough to Atlantic succeeded, made war on merchant shipping there. Success of GNEISENAU: Sank eleven and captured three ships with total of ca. 66,500 tons.
March 22, 1941:	Put in to Brest.
April 6, 1941:	Took air torpedo hit in stern during air attack.
April 10, 1941:	Hit by four bombs while in drydock, much damage and loss of personnel. Repaired until January 1942.
February 6, 1942:	Bomb near-miss while in dock.
February 11-13, 1942:	Operation "Cerberus", units at Brest (GNEISENAU, SCHARNHORST, PRINZ EUGEN) recalled to Germany to escape steadily increasing danger of air raids and base then in northern Norway in the future. Hit mine on the way, control reestablished after short time. Off Elbe mouth February 13, arrived in Kiel February 14, docked in floating dock at Deutsche Werke there.
February 26-27, 1942:	Took bomb hit in bow during night attack of British planes, glowing bomb splinters and pieces of iron from deck set fire to powder stored in "Anton" turret, explosion threw turret off its mount, whole bow burned out, 112 casualties. Decision made to transfer to Gotenhafen for repairs as well as rearmament.
April 4, 1942:	Under own power — escorted by training ship SCHLESIEN and icebreaker CASTOR — traversed icy Baltic Sea to Gotenhafen.
July 1, 1942:	Taken out of service.
January 1943:	All repair and rebuilding halted on order from Hitler and never resumed; all guns subsequently removed for use in coastal defense.
March 27, 1945:	Towed to Gotenhafen harbor entrance, there scuttled, on bottom as block ship.
As of 1947:	Broken up in Polish salvage operation, sealed and floated September 12, 1951, then completely scrapped.

Operation "Cerberus" began on February 11, 1942 with night departure from Brest in order SCHARNHORST — GNEISENAU — PRINZ EUGEN and, using surprise effect, traversed Straits of Dover in daylight, about noon on February 12. British countermeasures commenced only later, by use of destroyers and high-speed boats plus air attacks. All these attacks could be beaten off, causing the British some heavy losses. SCHARNHORST two mine hits, GNEISENAU one, but both units were able to continue the trip after a short time. On the same day the group reached its goal area in the German Bight. These pictures show the GNEISENAU during this undertaking.

Arrived in Kiel, the GNEISENAU docks at once; examination of the mine damage shows that it is not serious and can be repaired in two weeks, so she can be transferred to Norway as soon as possible. But it turns out differently: In the night of February 26, 1942 British bombers fly a routine attack and score a hit on the bow. After breaking through, the bomb hits a spot which gives access to the powder magazine below. Glowing bits of steel cause the powder to burn and explode. The shock lifts the "Anton" turret off its mount; it falls back as a burned-out shell. The bow is almost totally destroyed. 112 crewmen are killed. This air photo shows the GNEISENAU lying in the floating dock after the fatal attack.

All life in the bow is wiped out; this is how the bow looked when morning came. In the background is the typical shoreline scene in Kiel.

This very unclear photo nevertheless has documentary value: it shows the burned-out "Anton" turret that was just being removed.

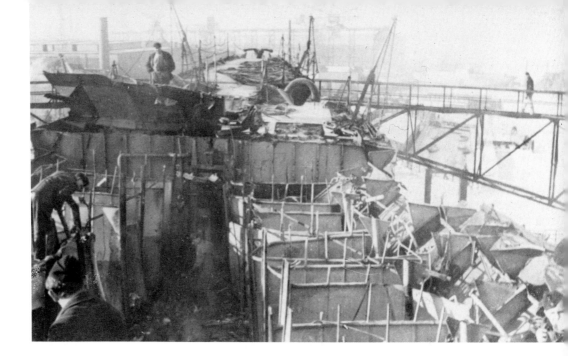

Seen from another angle: The destroyed bow, photographed during cleaning-out operations.

Repair work began at the Gotenhafen branch of the Deutsche Werke shortly after she arrived on April 4. One of the first operations was the removal of the three 28-cm triple turrets. While the "Anton" turret was only good for scrap iron, the other two turrets were taken to Norway and built into the rock in high places as coastal batteries, one each on Orland Peninsula at the entry to Trondheim Fjord and on Lille Sotra Island at the entrance to Bergen. Only the battery in the Trondheim area was finished by the end of the war. Of the medium artillery, two twin turrets and one single mantelet were set up at the northern tip of Fanö Island to block the entry to Esbjerg, the others were probably used on the Netherlands coast. In this picture taken by British air reconnaissance, the positions of the three turrets can be seen clearly. The removal of the bow is already in progress

In the floating dock at the Gotenhafen branch of the Deutsche Werke, the bow of the GNEISENAU was cut off. A floating crane beside her removes the parts to be used as scrap metal.

THE PLANNED REBUILDING

The fatal bomb hit sustained on February 26-27, 1942 gave the impetus to combining repairs with planned rearmament. The burnt-out bow was cut off at meter 187.5 of the ship's overall length — immediately before the "Anton" turret — and was to be replaced by a new one, ten meters longer at the design waterline, with its prow sharp almost all the way to the upper deck and without a bow bulge. This measure was necessary in any case because of the increased weight resulting from rearmament, as well as to give the bow more lift and correct the trim situation (resulting from several gains in weight during building, which had cost the GNEISENAU more and more freeboard, so that the upper edge of the side armor now was only about 1.20 meters above water at full displacement).

In planning the rebuilding, it was also to be ascertained whether the ship could be brought back to its originally calculated draught by widening, but in the end this had been ruled out, as the work time would have been even longer. Reinforcements and other constructive changes could not be left out, as they were needed to absorb the considerably greater recoil power of the larger caliber guns. In addition, changes also had to be made in the ammunition chambers. The planned heavy artillery consisted of six 38-cm guns in three twin turrets, as were in use on the battleships BISMARCK and TIRPITZ. The medium artillery and anti-aircraft guns were to remain unchanged.[1] It was planned to increase the machine weapons to six 20mm quadruple units and six 20mm single guns, a total of 30 barrels. Also part of the rearmament was the construction of the new airplane hangar, already done at Brest, as well as a new tripod mast that was to replace the mainmast behind the funnel; this had been shipped to Brest but it had not been possible to install it there. This would have made the GNEISENAU look very much like her sister ship, the SCHARNHORST. The total weight increase was calculated at about 1200 tons.

After rebuilding, the length at the design waterline would have been about 236.00 meters and the overall length about 245.00 meters. The standard displacement was calculated to have grown to 33,510 tons, the action displacement to 40,720 tons, and at the latter, the draught would have been 9.75 meters.

---

[1] Replacing the 15- and 105mm guns with new 128mm C/41 guns in (double-turret) C/41 rotating mantelets was also considered, but these thoughts were quickly discarded for a number of reasons.

When the flags were taken down and the ship taken out of service on July 1, 1942, it was taken for granted that a much stronger battleship could be put into action a year later. This hope could no longer be fulfilled. At the beginning of 1943 all work on the ship had to be stopped. This was decreed by the "Führer's order" of January 1943, which was very bad news for the Navy, as it ordered the large battle units, "useless" in Hitler's view, taken out of service. Thus the GNEISENAU remained hidden under camouflage nets in Gotenhafen. When the Red Army moved into the Danzig-Gotenhafen area, the ship was towed into the mouth of the harbor and set on the bottom there as a blocking ship. This picture shows the GNEISENAU with her stern lying on the bottom.

During the last phase of breaking up the ship. Of the superstructure, only the funnel, the armored command post and the barbettes of the forward turrets remained.

Taken on November 8, 1949: The wrecking cork on the battleship has progressed a long way. After the wreck had thus been lightened sufficiently, sealing the hull was begun. On September 12 it floated, and was immediately towed away to be scrapped.

NAVAL INFO UP-TO-DATE
INDIA'S NEW FRIGATES
A Symbiosis of Western and Eastern Naval Technology

India has had its own shipbuilding industry only since the mid-Sixties. This has been oriented to British maritime developments to the present, but recently Soviet naval technology has had a growing influence on it. A notable example of this consists of the GODAVARI class of frigates, begun in 1978 and continuing to 1983. In terms of naval architecture, they show typical style elements of the British LEANDER class to such an extent that they are regarded as being based considerably on that type. To be sure, these Indian frigates are somewhat longer and also wider than their British models. Their boiler system at least is also of British origin, as it consists of products of the firm of Babcock and Wilcox. No information is available as to the origin of the two drive turbine sets, but it cannot be ruled out that they may also come from British manufacturers.

The rocket weapons systems and the guns of the ship's artillery are of Soviet origin, as is the greater part of the electronic equipment. They consist of the following components:
* Four launching containers, each with one Soviet "SS-N-2C" sea target missile with a maximum range of 45 nautical miles (with no reloading possibility at sea).
* One "SA-N-4" short-range anti-aircraft rocket weapons system with a twin launching device and 20 rockets (fire control: a "pop-group" device).
* Two 57-mm ZIF-72 anti-aircraft guns in closed double mantelets (fire control: a "Muff Cob" device).
* Eight 30-mm AK 230 anti-aircraft guns in four double mantelets (fire control: two "Drum Tilt" devices).

The underwater weapons are of Italian origin. A-244S lightweight anti-submarine torpedoes of 324-mm diameter, made by Whitehead Motofides, are used, fired from permanently built-in sets of three tubes (American Mark 32 tubes made under license).

The electronics:
* A Soviet "MR-310" panoramic radar (NATO code designation "Head Net C") for sea and air surveillance at long range (air targets to 70, sea targets to 20 nautical mines); position: on the foremast.
* A "DA-08" panoramic radar made by Hollandse Signaal Apparaaten-Komzern (H.S.A.) of The Netherlands, for medium-range airspace surveillance; position: on the after mast.
* A British Type 978 radar by Decca Radar Ltd, for navigation; position: on the foremast.
* An Italian IPN-10 combat information system by Selenia Industrie Elettroniche.

The underwater orientation system comes from Great Britain; it is a Type 184M Panorama search-and-attack sonar by Graseby Instruments Ltd; position: on the bottom of the ship, some 25 meters from the bow.

The components of the flight system are a double hangar and the adjoining takeoff and landing pad. On the latter a "Beartrap" system made in Canada has been installed, with which it is possible to have the helicopter land safely on its platform, secure it against skidding in heavy seas, and move it in and out of the hangar safely. The British "Seaking" helicopter model is used in anti-submarine form; there is room in the hangar for two "Seakings", but only one is carried on board.

In terms of concept and design, this class obviously proves to be a successful symbiosis of western and eastern naval technologies. Now a new plan is in the offing: A design is being made in which a more marked "mix" of western and Soviet system components is planned. This so-called "Project 15" envisions a rocket frigate of about 5000 tons that can be regarded as a further development of the GODAVARI class and will be even more strongly equipped with weapons systems, sensors and elements of the power system of various origins.

Number of ships	3
Construction shipyard	Magazon Docks, Bombay
Standard displacement	3500 tons
Action displacement	4100 tons
Overall length	126.4 meters
Greatest width	14.5 meters
Draught (minus sonar dome)	4.5 meters
Main powerplant	2 gear-drive steam turbine sets
Power	30,000 horsepower (22,075 kW)
Boilers	2 Babcock & Wilcox 3-drum boilers, 38.7 atm pressure, at 450 degrees Celsius boiler temperature
Speed	27 knots
Range	4500 nautical miles at 12 knots
Sea-target rockets	4 "SS-N-2C" (4 containers)
Anti-aircraft rockets	20 "SA-N-4" (1 twin launcher)
Artillery	1 x 2 57-mm ZIF 72, 4 x 2 30- mm AK 230
Torpedo tubes	6 324-mm
Helicopter	1 "Seaking"
Crew	313 men

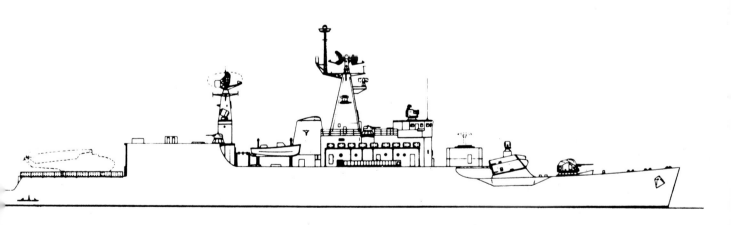

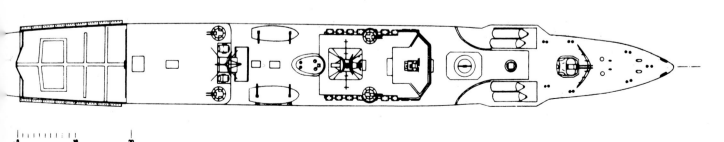

GODAVARI

The pyramidal mainmast carries the greater part of the sensors and antennae. On top is the Soviet "Head Net-2" panoramic radar, one level lower on the front the Type 978 navigational radar, plus other antennae. At the foot of the mast is the forward port 30-mm anti-aircraft twin, under it a row of escape pods.

The GODAVARI took part in the 1986 Liberty Review in New York; this full-length photo was taken there on July 3, 1986.

Before the New York skyline: the GODAVARI seen diagonally from forward. At the right edge of the picture is the 57-mm twin turret, on the side decks are the containers with the "SS-N-2C" sea-target rockets and their deflectors, between them the "Muff Cob" control device for the 57-mm anti-aircraft guns. In the area of the "SS-N-2C" containers the upper deck widens to the sides like a ramp to contain the needed space.

Seen from the other side: Behind the "SS-N-2C" containers the superstructure can be seen that contains the "SA-N-4" anti-aircraft rocket system. The launching device can move into and out of this. On the bridge is the "Pop Group" control device connected with it.

A view of the port side with the hangar area and the after mast, which carries the "DA-08" panoramic radar; below it is the after port 30-mm anti-aircraft twin. At left is one of the ship's boats, in the background the firing system for the submarine torpedoes.

A view diagonally from astern at the double hangar with the port overhead door open. The helicopter platform adjoins it at the right; its raised protective nets can be seen.

VEILED IN SECRECY: NORTH KOREA'S NAVY

No navy in the world is covered by such a thick veil of secrecy as that of North Korea. Its units obviously operate only in a narrow coastal zone and very rarely enter international waters, so that photos of them are very rare. Even in the traditional international fleet handbooks such as "Jane's Fighting Ships" and "Flottes de Combat" one can search in vain for actual photos. Yet this navy is certainly not small in terms of the number of its floating units; of course most of them are types that, by their size, were conceived only for action in coastal waters. This navy was established in the early Fifties of our century, after Korea was partitioned. Its first equipment consisted of vehicles and boats provided by the People's Republic of China and the Soviet Union. In more recent years the capacities of the North Korean shipbuilding industry, which is still very young, has grown to the point where, on the one hand, copies of certain Soviet and Chinese classes could be built and, on the other, their own developments could be realized (for which, of course, important components have been delivered, and still are, by both "big brothers"). As of about the middle of 1986, North Korea's navy is believed to have had the following strength:[1]

25 submarines (4 WHISKEY*, 4** + 12*** ROMEO, about 5 small submarines*** OF 41-meter length); 2 frigates (NAJIN*); 26 corvettes/subchasers (6* + 11*** SO-I, 2 TRAL*, 3 SARIWAN***, 6 HAINAN**); 32 high-speed rocket boats (8 SOJU***, 10 OSA-I*, 8 KOMAR*, 6 SOHUNG***); 136 high-speed torpedo boats (3 SHERSHEN*, 34 P-6*, 8 P-4*, 15 IWON***, 6 AN JU***, 70 KU SONG/SIN HUNG***); 167 motor gunboats (15 SHANGHAI-I/II**, 4 CHODO***, 4 K 48***, 20 MO-V*, 8 SHANTOU**, 66 CHAKO***, 40 CHONG JUNG***, 10 SIN PO***); 39 patrol boats (9 TAECHONG***, 10 KM-4*, 20 others); 128 landing craft (6 HANTAE***, 9 HANGCHOU***, 95 NAMPO*** and 18 LCM, in all 555 units.[2]

A few drawings from the East Asian area have been published recently, obviously originating from ship recognition service publications of the United States Navy that now have been made public. These and a few early photos may be sufficient to give a representative cross-section of this navy. The craft are almost exclusively North Korean developments, but some of them obviously are based on models from the "big brothers."

[1]* According to "Military Balance 1986-1987", p. 160. [2]* The asterisks indicate: * = from the Soviet Union, ** = from the People's Republic of China, *** = copies or original designs built in North Korean shipyards.

NAJIN class frigate, displacement 1200-1500 tons. Dimensions: 100 x 10 x 2.7 meters. Powerplant: Diesel engines. Speed: 25-26 knots. Armament: two 100-mm cannons, four 57-mm, four 25-mm and four 14.5-mm AA guns, three 533-mm torpedo tubes (replaced on one ship by a twin container group for "SS-N-2" sea-target rockets).

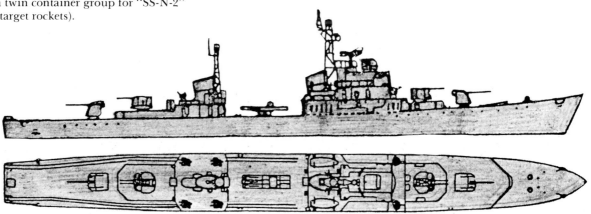

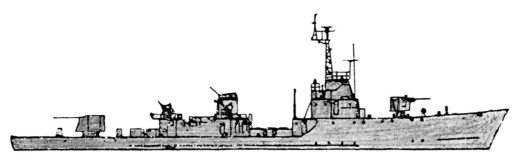

SARIWAN class corvette (modified copy of the Soviet
TRAL class of the Thirties). Displacement 475 tons.
Dimensions: 62.1 x 7.3 x 2.4 meters. Powerplant: Diesel
engines. Speed: 21 knots. Armament: two 57-mm, two
37-mm and six 14.5-mm AA guns.

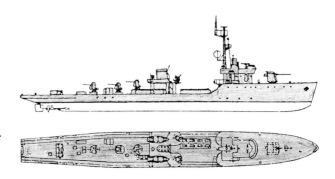

TRAL class corvette (ex-Soviet mineseeking
boats). Displacement 475 tons. Dimensions:
62.1 x 7.3 x 2.4 meters. Powerplant: Diesel
engines. Armament: one 100-mm cannon, three
37mm and four 14.5 AA guns.

TAECHONG class motor gunboat. Number: nine. Displacement: 140-165
tons. Dimensions: 44.2 x 5.5 x 2.4 meters. Powerplant: Diesel engines. Speed:
15 knots. Armament: two 57-mm, one 37-mm, four 25-mm and four 14.5-mm
AA guns and two anti-submarine RBU-1200 rocket launchers.

CHODO motor gunboat. Displacement: 130-... tons. Dimensions: 42.7 x 5.8 x
2.6 meters. Powerplant: Diesel engines. Speed: 24 knots. Armament: one 76-
mm cannon, two 37-mm and two 14.5-mm AA guns.

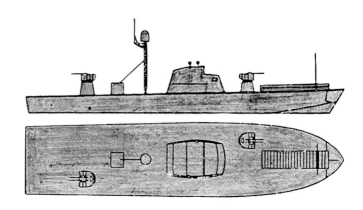

NAMPO class landing craft. Rebuilt Soviet P-6
torpedo boat type. Displacement: 82-... tons.
Dimensions: 27.7 x 6.1 x 1.8 meters. Powerplant:
Diesel motors. Speed: 40 knots. Speed: 40 knots.
Armament: four 14.5-mm AA guns. Obviously only
for personnel transport.

HANCHON class landing craft. No other data
available.

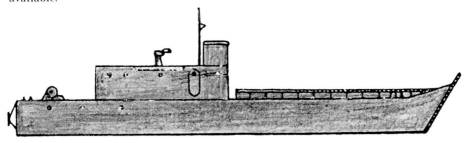

The drawings are not
reproduced here in the
same scale!

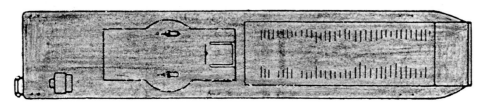

SO-I class subchaser (North Korean version). Displacement: 170-215 tons. Dimensions: 42.4 x 6.1 x 1.8 meters. Powerplant: Diesel engines. Speed: 28 knots. Armament: one 85-mm cannon, two 37-mm and four 14.5-mm AA guns.

K 48 class motor gunboat. Displacement: 110 tons. Dimensions: 38.1 x 5.5 x 1.5 meters. Powerplant: Diesel engines. Speed: 24 knots. Armament: one 76-mm cannon, three 37-mm and two 14.5-mm AA guns.

KM-4 class patrol boat. Displacement lo tons. Dimensions: 14.0 x 3.2 x 0.9 meters. Powerplant: Diesel engines. Armament: one 37-mm and one 14.5-mm AA guns.

NEW FRIGATE SERIES FOR THE ROYAL NAVY

A new British frigate series is presently underway. The six units of the so-called "Batch 2" of the British BROADSWORD class represent a modified variant that differs essentially from the first four ships. Among other things, they are some 14 meters longer, giving them a greater sea durability, more space for submarine tracking systems and better seaworthiness. This class will be followed by four further-improved craft as "Batch 3", the first of which is to be put into service in 1987.

The six units of "Batch 2" are as follows:
BOXER (F 92), in service 1984;
BEAVER (F 93), in service 1984;
BRAVE (F 94), in service 1985;
LONDON (F 95), planned for 1987;
SHEFFIELD (F 96), planned for 1987;
COVENTRY (F 97), planned for 1988.
Displacement: 4200/4800 tons (standard/maximum)
Main dimensions: 145 or 146.5 meters length, 14.75 meters beam, 6.0 meters draught maximum
Powerplant: Gas turbines producing total of 65,280 HP for speed of 30 knots.
Armament: 4 MM-38 "Exocet" sea-target rocket launchers, 2 sixfold rocket launchers for "Sea Wolf" anti-aircraft rockets, 2 40-mm AA guns, 6 submarine 324-mm torpedo tubes, 2 "Lynx" subchasing helicopters.